Navigating a Terrifying *Paradise*

Caitlin Pianta

Dedicated to making poor choices
and the ensuing character growth.

TABLE OF CONTENTS

PART ONE 1

NAVIGATING A TERRIFYING PARADISE 1

STORMS AT MY WINDOWS 2
RETURN 3
CHAOS 4
PIN DROP SUNDAY 5
VIOLET 6
MOONSICK 7
INTO THE NIGHT 8
UNKIND HABITS 9
SING SONG 10
INDENTATIONS 11
DRAUGHT 12
SILENCE 13
BAD FAITH ACTOR 14
WHISPERED HOUR 15
LOAN 16
GOOD SHIP PIRATE 17
DARK SODA 18
PUPPY 19

PART TWO 20
HERE IN THE EMBERS AT THE END OF THE WORLD, WE LANGUISH, EXCHANGING CORPOREAL PLEASANTRIES 20
VULNERABLE 21
FLIGHT OF THE BUTTERFLIES 22
BLANKET 23
SUSTENANCE 24
ACCIDENTAL PHANTOMS 25
DRAGONS 26
TO BE YOUR POET 27
GARDEN #1 28
THORNS 29
TOURIST 30
PRIMARY COLOURS 31
STORYTELLING 32
GHOST 33
INERTIA 34
DIFFERENT WINTERS 35
ETERNAL STALEMATE 36
ROMANTIC DISTANCE 37
MONSTERS 38
TEMPORARY MOTHER 39
TO BE MY POET 40
INFERNO 41

PART THREE 42

THE BITTER END IS WHAT YOU MAKE OF IT, LIKE, NO MORE EGGS FOR BREAKFAST 42

    TIL DEATH 43

    YES, YOU AREN'T 44

    HIBERNATE 45

    MUSE AND CURE 46

    IMAGINATION 47

    ANCHOR 48

    PINE 49

    ANTIQUE 50

    LUCID DREAMING 51

    GRACELESS 52

    SNOW DRIFT 53

    SPACES 54

    WORDS JUMPED OFF THE PAGE 55

    POLLUTION 56

    VANILLA 57

    SCAFFOLD 58

    EARTHQUAKES UNDERNEATH 59

PART FOUR 60

ALONG DAINTY LINES WE WALTZ A WITTY REPARTEE, MY SUMMER RACONTEUR BECOMES MY WINTER MEMORY 60

    AUTUMN 61

    SLEEP DEBT 62

SKULL	63
TANGO	64
FABRIC	65
GARDEN #2	66
BLEACHERS	67
WAKING UP	68
IN CONVERSATION	69
HEIGHT OF SUMMER	70
MORNING OF JUST ME	71

PART FIVE 72

A WINCE EVOLVED INTO AN EARTHQUAKE, WAIF OF A WOMAN, REBUILT IN STONE. 72

HAIR	73
ACKNOWLEDGEMENTS	74

PART ONE
NAVIGATING A TERRIFYING PARADISE

STORMS AT MY WINDOWS

There aren't enough storms at my windows.
These days, I create them
With harvested grapes, fermented in jars and
Making my own fun —

Deciphering handwriting on letters
Passed to each other from seats far apart,
Back when our love was built with
Ambitions to last —

Then construction paused and we drowned in the storm
Of the routine of performative chaos we caused.

Salmon and eggs and drinking all day
On a Sunday.
One day, the pattern, the ballet will change, they
Say it's the sunlight
You let in that matters the most, but I'm too quick
To sell out for the rain.

RETURN

Restlessness erodes as fast as it grows and some promised potential whispers in prose.
Don't ask where I've been or whether I've eaten, I scarcely recall the desire to repeat it.

Slowly, my stories become nothing more than wild gesticulations howled from the floor,
re-told over lines on the kitchen counter of some budget motel I can barely afford.

You cast your eyes down because you hear my foot tapping, nails rapping on the table, words clipped by impatient teeth —

So gently, so sweet you make a plan to release and I don't spare a thought for your patience with me —

So, you send me away to nap on foreign couches, on indigo lounges like a cat in the sun, paws stretched to the window, to whatever winds may blow for however long lasts the impression of fun.

But I'll escape through the night, through the streets, dodging light, to return to your door and scratch at the frame —

You leave it ajar, if a little too far, for when food gets scarce, I return to you again.

CHAOS

Chaos knocked; once, twice at my door,
And I relented,
Invited him in for a banquet,
Spilled wine on myself and could only say thank you.

Dragged me to the eye of the storm, calm and violent.
I liked it.
For too long a while, I imbibed it.

Chased my tale through these cities,
Gutters papier-mâchéd
By good money and bad, I've made
And discarded,
Just to have moonbeams jam my eyes and those violent suns rise,

An alcoholic reprise
The landscape of this life.

NAVIGATING A TERRIFYING PARADISE

PIN DROP SUNDAY

Pin drop Sundays, I can barely stand it — acres of silence
I'd rip my skin off to escape.

Restless isolation on the horizon of my life — the smell of
cities fled, smouldering ruins in my wake.

Grew up to take the bait, fell straight into a latent rage.
All the fate I waited to embrace looked fake outside the
cage.

Unsated, then agitated and then we come unchained.

Feckless Fridays, strobe light Saturdays, blood of my
victims on my chin — stalking doorways of past allies, not
one to let me in—

Dissent to anger, violent fall into the pit of hate I'd grown
— crushed bones of the bodies left paved the coop I'd
flown —

Alone on voiceless acres; till the soil, reap what I've sown
— these solitary Sundays, now, and how I've come to
know them.

The punishing calm, cold harm after the violence — so
quiet outside my mind, and I can't stand the silence —

Dropping pins to hear the ring, when once I heard the riot.

VIOLET

This scent of violet, soft threaded violence
Through slightly cracked window, brought on the back of howling winds —

Such ghostly things

That bring you back into my life again.

A little-known soul, faint evening takes hold,
Sweeps in waves to brush memories through soft curls of red hair —

Between life and death

Is the sway of the mystery that keeps us all there.

Fall peaceful to sleep, dreamscape within reach,
Vibrations of violet bring blue hues of belief —

The wind falls to peace.

And as hushed as you arrived, you softly take your leave.

MOONSICK

Moon, Master of Tides;
Influencer of souls,
I'll follow where you guide,
Relinquish control

Of dreams, you provide
Ever waning night light,
Dictating the goals
Set by mankind.

I get tan lines
From your glow,
Reflecting on past lives
Sitting in the window,

Flowers grow on dark vines
World in black and white —
Here, silently, is where I
Wait for Romeo.

Abate sore heart woes —
Moon sick lunatic,
Stuck in the throes
Of racing thoughts, it

Could be I've flown
Too close to the night, thick
With stars and clouds sewn
Into moonlit fabric.

INTO THE NIGHT

Compel me into the night — where I belong.
Imprinted paws on pavement, stalking the doors of grave
mistakes to chase rabbit holes of selfish gains.

Morbid fires, recalcitration of sin — let me in, let me in.
I've been all alone
And I'm dying in Eden.

Discarded bird carcass — hollow bones
Fluttered heart,

Bacon in oil on buttered toast,
And nowhere safe to fall apart.

UNKIND HABITS

I kept unkind habits in glass jar collections,
Labelled with affections,
Prepared for the fall;
For in shameful impact with marble tile floor

I break once,

And then,

I break once more.

SING SONG

Lay here and listen to the rain —
A-frame house,
Quiet as a mouse.
Same old dream on replay but I can't say what it's about.

Lay here and hope the morning comes —
Never know if
This will be it,
There's only one sun and it won't always be lit.

In a sing song voice in my head —
Nursery rhyme verse,
Trundling hearse.
Ring Around the Rosie and we all fall down dead.

Trying to take a breath through my nose —
All stuffed up,
Lungs puffed up.
Respiratory distress as ragged as my prose.

Tried to write a story you would like —
It always turns out,
What I write about
Is really just for me and what I see after life.

INDENTATIONS

Rain fell like merciful bullets, lifted the steam out of our skin with gentle kisses, and easy.
The ledge you held me on, perched on instinct, with just your arm around my waist.

Before the rain subsided, you left this taste — then you were gone.

With glazed eyes, engaged in conversations I could not kick or bluff my way out of — the air in the room you left behind was braille indentations of your prior presence, and thickly it hung — wrested from my lungs, stolen away in that moment.

Months in quiet contemplation, when time is more contentedly spent in isolated daydreams — rain and music take on new meanings, the kind that doesn't need tactile fulfilment — fodder for my soul, glowing skin where summer raindrops struck holes.

Seasonal shift brings you into focus, three-dimensional lust as you thrust off the page — once a canvas of letters in independent language, now a striking mural of violent, primary paint.

How dare I attempt to trace, with reticent fingers, the hidden movements of your life — delicate, the dance becomes to keep you by my side —

Yet I chase your braille indentations to sate the riot in my mind.

DRAUGHT

Wind blows through the corridors of my vacant heart.
Then it starts; the slow, rhythmic closing of doors to
capture the draught.

There it stays, trapped — tornadoes rip across maps of cleft
veins and meaty ventricles — Impulses electrical pulsate
through my physical to become my theoretical,

While butterflies paint the walls of my stomach in vomit.

I bathe in the disquiet my genetic inheritance has promised
me —
We could flee, look at me.

If you see in my eyes the same exhausted reprise,
Keep it a secret, between you and I.

NAVIGATING A TERRIFYING PARADISE

SILENCE

Your silence whispers.
Pours toxins into the gaps in my attachment.
My hinges are rusting.
Deciding in resolute disgust to never love again…

But tinnitus rings.
You're here again.
Stoking fire from the dull tones of my distress,

I burn.

Silence will return again,

A bittersweet present you would gift me for days,
No way to live,
But love finds a way.

BAD FAITH ACTOR

The knives are somewhere, missing, all the spoons escaped their draws — there's prints across the floor, muddy creatures' paws whose jaws are clenched and anxious sores.

I am in the bathroom bowing, as the cosmic curtain closes — an orchestra of roses thrown at the feet of the composer.

Closure in the mirror, smashed, a million shards of glass that I am pulling out of me, like all your infected parts.

Failing immune system in the intestines, racked and manic — attacked by panic, mouth full of blood cells and a cup that runneth over.

How we longed for each other in the spaces between bank tellers' fingers — where paper lingers, every fibre a metaphor for systems infinitely bigger.

For what we will be doing behind the veil of presentation, the intake of breath before the final hesitation?

I say you will be picking me out of your teeth for years.

NAVIGATING A TERRIFYING PARADISE

WHISPERED HOUR

In this whispered hour, what's become of you, of us —
when trust met betrayal, will this tale outlive us now?

Will it be cast to dust, with whatever else we've left —
words you litter carelessly fill the chasm in my chest.

To the crackling soundtrack of the fire as you light it — I
wither on the vine of my own life, pretend to like it,

Flames climb the burning wreck of all that we have been —
and I flee before you see the ashen prints that stain my
cheeks.

Two steps closer, a step too close — suspend me in this
moment — above the cement and right before the fall,
wrapped in a bow, and

I post my eloquence away, if you could only save it for the
day, I can digest this world enough to then return to you
and claim it.

LOAN

In the liminal space between your love
I extend the loan of our time,
Pulling lines of credit from behind exhausted eyes.

Together in line, sometimes alone,
I watch you slip home between moving paths,
How reality splinters beneath the weight of your heart.

GOOD SHIP PIRATE

Walked into your gin joint, synced energies — the good ship pirate — glass extracted from envious eyes of onlookers, and we imbibed it —

Drank deep into a night that rolled over steampunk waves of cogs and buckles — bloody knuckles — fought every ghost that stepped up to haunt you, dear.

Oath of blood on the galley floor — gallery of stories — moon eclipsing on my thighs, heart full of petrol fires and glory.

A plea to break the curse, promised slipknot in rope around my wrists — kissed deeply — cast the fishing net of my dress to the abyss.

Cement packed heart and this aching cavity — the good ship pirate — sunk through leagues of oil set in foreboding tones of black.

Let the tide rip through my body, rush me to the trough below — so you may sail, but as you know — sunrise will chase you back to me and my discarded ghost.

DARK SODA

Dark soda hangover and the liquor it was mixed with — gifted last Christmas, hanging off the fridge beside the kitchen — flinging silver coins into the abyss beside the hinges.

In the cold, fresh middle distance on the window pane, an imprint — the last shards of glass I'm left with, under the languorous pause of finite distance.

Dark soda hangover, slid from wall to floor — found comfort in linoleum — stayed for a year or more.

Watched the doorway intersect, crucified against the jamb — dragged by my neck and by my hands,

Until you wanted me again.

NAVIGATING A TERRIFYING PARADISE

PUPPY

I'm a puppy under your table.
How the tables have turned — how the embers were stoked into a fire that burned.

Scar tissue on my chest, scalpel cut away the flesh — stand back from your handiwork, admire what you've left.

Got half a heart and full intentions, beg like a dog for your attention — submitted my confessions, pull the leash and teach your lessons — on my best behaviour, never waiver for acceptance —

Used to have this energy, what else can you take from me — loyal to a fault until you threw me off the balcony.

Doused in this naivety; sit, stay, beg and kick the bowl to me — leftovers for the well behaved is all you'll ever be for me.

PART TWO

HERE IN THE EMBERS AT THE END OF THE WORLD, WE LANGUISH, EXCHANGING CORPOREAL PLEASANTRIES

VULNERABLE

Remind me — what are we doing here?
Knees bowed over the armrest,
Thighs holding your beer.

Between the coffee table and the couch
I'm folded like a paper crane,
My thumb contorts my mouth.

Brush the hair out of my eyes and smile.
Say something like, "You're lovely,
I can only stay a while."

Fridge is buzzing from the kitchenette,
Blue light from the television,
Shadows puddle on my neck.

Remind me — what are we meant to do?
Was never meant to be this drunk
And dumb and vulnerable with you.

FLIGHT OF THE BUTTERFLIES

This requited, all-encompassing flight of the butterflies —
soft wings brush internal walls — flutter through
passageways, Winter migration, stomach to heart.

Two insomniacs, you steal my sleep for safekeeping — to
make use of later, when I have need to escape —

Cocoons discarded with time, lost to the gradual ache of
words — brushed lip compensation — drape patterned
wings over cool September skin.

When we take flight again into daylight confrontation, what
mural of our evenings will imprint new colour strains?

BLANKET

Your lips could always quiet mine on afternoons like this — inside a room so cold we'd need the extra blanket — from the top shelf of the cupboard, the tall cupboard with the mirror — the one where we would watch ourselves watching for each other.

Keep our skin warm by gentle measures, drape my body over yours — a whole sea of night exploding, the way a new universe is born.

Always awake a little earlier than you, but I would wait for you to join — keeping questions just behind my teeth, in the warmth beneath my tongue.

Then your fingers reach for the thermostat stuck to the wall inside my heart — try to kick you out of my head, or at least my bed, but find I can't.

And how you like it cold, so you can drape my body over yours —

Just like the blanket from the top shelf of the cupboard with the mirror — the one where I could watch you watch us as we watched for each other.

SUSTENANCE

Lean against off-white, faux leather couch front,
Sitting on the floor,
And I fold into you, like corners,
Like you hold me up and still —

Eighteen months in the making, we eat dumplings with our hands,
And talk about the weather,
The way that only those familiar can,
      Like high pressure wind systems through the Bight in May.
When we'd abandon to the ocean, the words we'd rather say.

I feel your eyes follow me as I put lotion to my skin,
Then here we are again,
Your face angled up toward me, fragile,
      Like the leaves, late Autumn season,
         Succumbing to new Winter's breeze.

How we give each other words,
Without forming speech to lips,
And how the world does not exist
On days of sustenance like this.

ACCIDENTAL PHANTOMS

Here, there's phantoms we created with the friction of our skin; the walls are thin — our hearts are thick with patience from letting the bad things in —

Confessions pinned to our lapels in anxious languages, obscure — step beyond the city limits when the storm drains start to overflow —

With clumps of flesh ripped from my chest in desperate handfuls, brutal nails — drug through a body built on chalkboard dust and hail,

As we set down the tools we gave each other, but never learned to use — before the world that overtook us spun too far out of our view —

But the fog still falls on windows of the lives we didn't choose — we couldn't make — and all these accidental phantoms we created slowly fade.

DRAGONS

Watching the colour come back into the cheeks of the forest
With the sunrise,

Smoke, like the shadows of dragons,
Reflects on the snow.

The call and response of our fingers
Through a window,

Some remote town poised between antique mountains,
Stringing troubles on pink cherry blossom strands,
Dancing between stark tree branches, like bread crumbs,
I trace your steps from snow to sand.

TO BE YOUR POET

It's nothing new, flying kites at night on the beach — with you just out of reach — I'm here, underneath the Evening Star, obscured by the clouds of wherever you are.

Yes, time goes quickly — weaving in and out of days, leaving such little trace — but that's okay, time is as make believe as the things we see on the vacant beach after too many drinks —

I always see you.

Rattle loose the pictures in my head, the only trinkets I collect — lay them in straight lines on my bed, backwards chronology set to a canvas I paint red — subconscious art, not realised yet — oh, to be your poet —

Fictional fingers of time beckon me to go — all the things I do not know become keys, attract electric current flow — grip tighter silver scissors, swallowed fear of the unknown —

So, cut loose tame kite — released into the ocean winds of night, alone — no starlight strong enough to illuminate the dark path home.

GARDEN #1

Where does the smoke go
When it escapes your dying cigarette,
And out the window,

Where it blows through the air above my head,

Where I sit,
I've been waiting in your garden all these years,

Such a precarious balance
That I service so patiently.

NAVIGATING A TERRIFYING PARADISE

THORNS

All the things I'd trade for you pirouette away from me — teasing me, if you'd believe in me, we could seize the symphony,

You learn the violin for me, I write our Opus — hopeless though it may be, play something in a minor key — hollow out the inside of me — scoop the soul right out of me —

It's nothing new, strings plucked of a primaeval tune — but I'm unique to you, and you to my heart, too — the little death that I would give to you rendered in the music soon.

Bring the chaos we were birthed of to my door — we've known the pain of patience before, as around us fertile garden grew tall — and now —

Hidden from the modern gaze — we're lost among the roses…and their thorns.

TOURIST

Considering the last time
When the wine was running low,
Remnant droplets chasing light down upturned curvatures
of glass,
Onto moist and tipsy tongues
To turn their keys in locks behind our teeth,
Pull our words from dusty locket hearts
To fade before us as we speak.

But you're a tourist through my winter,
How your coat brushes my skin
With the vocabulary of your movement
And the patterns of your sins.

PRIMARY COLOURS

As our chorus rises, fractures the new light of the dawn —
soft, pale angles pressed against picture painted skin, with
nothing on — we're primary colours now.

Hours dry on the walls, blank white canvas witness —
flush with brush strokes conjured by familiar movements,
smooth — and those fingertips play freckled notes, skip
over exposed hip bone chords.

Bathed in blankets, unseasonably cool November — sifting
stories through trivial mementos, of our past.

Calm voice glides forward to meet inviting ears — cutting
clear against the outside influence, competing footsteps and
faint speech — but here,

Where our chorus rises, where canvas comes to brush —
just for us, and the primary colours we've become.

STORYTELLING

When we lie in bed, your leg under mine, your words playing melodies,
Stretching the strings within my mind,
Tracing fingers through your chest hairs,
Over scars you've come to find
Through the journeys of your life that I don't know a thing about,
I don't need to know about,
But, how long we've both known drought.

I like to read in bed, crack the spine of your book, among our blanket ocean,
Somewhere where they cannot look,
Peruse the gamut that our natures run,
Embracing the paths we took
Through the days that lead us here, that we don't talk about,
We don't need to talk about,
But that we would not be here without.

Then, in gentle tones, share a story of your life, without really speaking,
Where does she think you are tonight?
The reasons for escape are woven threads into these sheets,
Written on our sleeves,
Hidden in our sleep, where we would always dream about
How the rain would flood the drought,
And how our gardens flourish now.

GHOST

Across each other's landscapes we chase the ghost of our
potential — a greyscale day, distressed by rain, torrential
— our chaos reigns, its savage bliss lays siege upon the
terrain of this hotel room—

And how do you, dear chaos, beat your drum inside our
chests — uneven footing beneath, this bed — we make the
most of what is left — with clenched fist impatience we
draw the moat bridges inside our heads.

This that will not be confessed — the watered, rotting roots
of our potential —
the gut-wrenching roller coaster; love me never or forever,
still — those decayed flowers, spooked, by what? We
cannot tell —as we manifest our misbeliefs and retreat into
ourselves.

And you, dear chaos — a sunrise escapes out of my door
— the last of your shadows loosen their grip — seep their
grey from the carpet on the floor.

So, here I lay, forever, for a while and then some more —
in the quiet aftermath of the legacy of our war.

INERTIA

Sluggish opposition to change under a blanket, ignorant bliss found right where I left it —

I'm trying to give you no sudden moves to react to, you know I'd walk beside you — slowly, and forever, a few steps behind you,

So you don't scatter away, dissipate, again, over the rolling, green ocean to the Southern winds.

Socks slung over your heart while I shower, if only they'd anchor you, here, firm in this tower, this palace we've built in the bed we devour —

The ballast of my head and the ache of inertia, right where I want it, on this pillow I've searched for,

For longer than I've known you, or kept you at all, the threat of loss closes in faster than ever before.

NAVIGATING A TERRIFYING PARADISE

DIFFERENT WINTERS

I return from you damaged —
We remember different Winter nights, an evening coloured
by the season and those crisp and crunchy skies.

We watched city skyline views from the antique turret in
the park — and in an ocean of warm light, our isolated isle
of dark.

Dirt under my fingernails —
As I tore grass carpet apart, bruised,
Like fruit clung to a vine too long and spoon-fed you blood
like juice.

Passers-by cast curious eyes, ill-adjusted to the night — the
collage we create, part freeze but mostly flight.

This landscape is a maze —
My memory floods with smoke and mirrors, may I see
behind the cloak, and may I tend your wounds forever.

ETERNAL STALEMATE

Beauty when you don't speak, meet your eyes and they mirror, eternal stalemate — reflected harsh truth, half-truths —

We build a castle in the dark. A monument to this half-hearted, hardly love.

To the point of breaking, to the point of saying this — trade the harmless grey of limbo and how it blankets everything —

Out the window, where the night remains. One thing you cannot touch.

These fingertips you have, where did you steal them from — cannot scare me when we do wrong,

There was a minor chord inside our song — an abyss where we belong.

ROMANTIC DISTANCE

Content posture, fingers circling through neglected headboard dust — a romantic distance maintained between us, I hear our music —

Off-beat intimacy, bass clef assurances — only a moment away, you lie in maiden feathered pillows — comfortably buried in the softest hallways of my heart.

Planting flowers on the parallels we find — where our stories intersect and then diverge, I'm not her — yet you populate my mind —

Ideas pollinating words, the bee frollicks between the birds — and I'm a mirror to this world, so I guess pain can be reversed.

Surely you were born with a novel inside your head — on selfish evenings we close the distance and read together in our beds —

I point to stars, and name them, the constellations of our frailties — across this romantic distance, where I wait for you to embrace this.

NAVIGATING A TERRIFYING PARADISE

MONSTERS

The clatter of the shower as you slide open the door, elephant beats of bass stomp down from the floor above us — you step over the lip of tiles, leave footprint imprints as you walk — the towel, a haphazard handkerchief posing as a shawl —

Hangs off you like an adoring fan, taught to leave your skin a damp and perfect canvas for the droplets dripping from your elbows to your hands.

I see a devil on your shoulder, but how much does he really know — empty vessel between his fingers that linger on the leftovers of my soul — ghostly as it is, to live between heaven and hell — what secrets he could whisper, we could surely never tell.

The moisture on your lips transfers to the skin across my chest — travels south to bone bridged sternum, north to pale and tender neck —

Surely the monsters can't dance forever on the wall above our bed, pushed against the window, where seasons start to shed —

And though I know we shouldn't be here, well, the monsters must be fed.

TEMPORARY MOTHER

Your geometry, crushed and crumpled beneath my fingers,
I watch you rise and fall,
In a return to something primal that we surely knew before,
The deep cut writing
On the soft womb wall.

How you fall apart in my hands, and how I weave you back together,
Melted onto me like a Dali,
I become a temporary mother,
In a temporary home,
Built of our blood and bone.

Slipping through the openings
Between shaking shoulders,
Breaking edges of your fragility,
To bathe you like a son,
The sun,
The son I rose in you.

How we evolved to love, I keep you on my breast —
Against a matte black headboard,
The wall above, with one palm pressed,
To feel the heartbeat of this house,
To see your heartbeat as you rest.

TO BE MY POET

You became my poetry,
My symphony.
Reached in to pluck the heart from me,
Strings vibrate on harp of bone.

I rehearse your verse, stray from home,
You find me in the wilderness,
Scattering our words
To the bears, to the birds,

To soften the edges of the world.

INFERNO

The skies cast in periwinkle blue,
As the devil read Dante's "Inferno", enthused,
Beside my bathtub
And out loud.

I submerged into a liquid pool of galaxies,
Wailed of what you meant to me,
Wrapped my hands around our future as it fled into black holes.

Remember, we danced with such abandon
Through the hallways of hotels,
Planned to meet again in hell, we said,
When all was said and done.

Now, in loose skyscraper homes beside me
I stack nursery rhymes and fantasies,
Hair kinked into flawed footholds,
Built for you to climb.

Well, if you're ever so inclined.

PART THREE

THE BITTER END IS WHAT YOU MAKE OF IT, LIKE, NO MORE EGGS FOR BREAKFAST

NAVIGATING A TERRIFYING PARADISE

TIL DEATH

As hands paint invisible pictures through the air above where our knees touch, we smile,
With teeth and gums,
I scrape the plate for crumbs of your details.

Hungry years stretched behind us as we fell on couches before fireplaces to state our cases,
Swap our stories,
Waited for the pauses so I could speak.

We moved through painted rooms and kept fish behind glass inside our walls, peppered their ceilings,
Put fingers to the panes to help them trace
An illusion of an unfamiliar path inside their cage.

As days slipped away between the couch cushions, eyes that watched us eat and sleep and natter,
Our words from so long ago haunted the hallways of our home,

Always love you,
Always need you,
Always feed you.

But what happens when my appetite is sated and the only dream I have left to whittle away the long hours in your company is fantasising where I would dispose of your corpse?

YES, YOU AREN'T

Words move around my mouth, brush my teeth — grating enamel off to flake into my throat

And collect in tiny castles of what we should have spoken.

But we posed in photos, with skin touching through clothes — trying not to pay attention to the history of our prose.

Now the gap in conversation grows — we don't ask after each other, anymore — through mutual friends in bored, suburban streets,

With cold drinks in our hands and hot bitumen under our feet.

So, it's standing against walls, avoiding weeds, building homes in flaws — because, it should have been your floor, like it was before.

This unique taste, yes, you aren't mine anymore.

HIBERNATE

Let me show you
How to walk away.

If we do it slowly,
Allow our love to hibernate,
It may survive the winter,

May thrive in splintered
Vines through concrete tiles

We can tread upon,
One day, again, as friends.

MUSE AND CURE

Let me linger slightly longer on the muse from late December — what lit the fuse, I can't remember, but never will I ash the ember —

Let me ponder while we wander through the hotel hallways, drunk — when the bombshell of our lust exploded, it took out towns and city blocks.

When my envy filled my empty soul, spilled onto bedroom floors — I'll usurp who groomed your heart before, to brave the theatre of your war —

And you tempered what had angered me in seasons long since past — what reason your glance was this way cast, I will not tempt the fates to ask —

What is tonight if not a fight to stay in your arms I will not win — how beautiful you are in Spring, how sure you are of everything —

If the world should end unfurl your hand in mine up on the balcony, here — what brought our minds to meet, my dear, may never be exactly clear —

As long as you linger slightly longer on our cure from late December — what repaired my soul, I can't remember, but never will I forget the splendour.

IMAGINATION

Look at me. My question burns a hole in my oesophagus,
All the oxygen was taken,
Nothing left for the rest of us.

You know death intimately. I've never died at all.
Trying to come of age
Without succumbing to the thrall.

Skim the edge of insanity enough to dip my feet, see,
All my baggage is in boxes,
As I divorce reality.

Learnt how to leave before I learnt object permanence,
Let my imagination run wild —
But it always gathers at the fence.

ANCHOR

Vast darkness cast me out, this mastless ship — direction unacquired — and silent sea surrounding me, I've tried to be free within your tide.

Eulogising life, before and after all what was it for — a scratch in time, a single line, a futile, frozen, catch twenty-nine.

Thirty next; no rest or pause — wrested from my brittle claws — I cannot find the words to cause, link my sequence of effects to yours.

What's more, I'm empty of allegory — all literal when I transcribe the story — it's raw but scarcely relatable, what fate exists is left untraceable.

From afar, nautical star, listless navigator above:

Guide me away
from love.

NAVIGATING A TERRIFYING PARADISE

PINE

I know of enough words that may begin to touch your eyes
— describe to me a life, brick walls around a sunlit room
— the world may fall to ruin around us, as long as there
was me and you —

But somewhere in the evening breeze, nesting in the
promised leaves of change — (how they refused to fall) —
Autumnal love always eluded me.

The forest grew around, stamped tepid embers out to cold
and swept the ash toward the ocean — the way our
promises were broken, fast and callous and unspoken.

I found myself cast out, drunk on a baffling evening of self
— following a broken compass to a wilderness beyond the
dark — to sit in solitude, promises wilting on their vines —

Whole forests will be demolished in service of my pining
heart.

ANTIQUE

Straying over uneven seaside pavement — a winding, wounded snake cutting dark ribbons down the coast — uncharted nautical star, radiant and misleading — not found on any map, yet it lures me out to sea —

Each light in every window, the potential of a home — these cautious feet continue toward the tense magnetic pull — of anguished, antique winds spiced with the salt of foreign shores.

The night, a cup tipped over — silken starlight pours like milk to pause on Dresden skin.

These familiar hands dance over freckled constellations, alabaster composition under artists fingertips —

Quiet breaths of apprehension, though content in steady pace, still; how the map can be redrawn, how the stars can be so faithful —

How confused hearts can find a place fused in some fate they were unsure of.

NAVIGATING A TERRIFYING PARADISE

LUCID DREAMING

You're a pterodactyl and I'm a land-locked reptile, your wings can take you anywhere — I didn't leave my room last year.

Violin, play me memories, make me a sinner, make me enemies — leave calluses on my fingers and blood running down the bow.

Wake me up and while I'm drowsy, between the dream and the reality — help me weave a web of words that can live up to our memories.

Play in the stream of consciousness, stay in the dream of a conscience that tumbleweeds across a playground so far beyond my means —

Make the whole thing clear, less obscene than things I've seen — in the rolling dice of waking life, confined to its narrow seams.

GRACELESS

The ease with which tears tease my lashes these days, it's astounding. There used to be rooms I'd be proud to be found in.

But I've outgrown those spaces, uncomfortable couches — these gangly limbs passing from plate to mouth —

As I grow, I don't know a way back through the doorway, confined to this tiny room.

Carved hollow roads through marrow and bone, ran out of space for sadness to call home, anymore —

Cannot seek restful sleep on the floor, so it paces, curls into a ball, whimpers, graceless — like an unwanted dog I've abandoned before —

Trips me up on my way out of bed.

The worms find a home in my heart, who could blame them, we're all the same and there's no shame in Eden — they start to party, it's all just confetti.

We nourish ourselves for the grave.

NAVIGATING A TERRIFYING PARADISE

SNOW DRIFT

Where others flee, I have found comfort.
Remember me,

When dark clouds gather to battle righteous suns;
But give up on the crest,
Fall in love, build a nest,
And spend the days throwing scribbled notes toward the ocean.

Give me a recipe:
A long day ahead and not much to do.
I may spend it confusing my pain with love for you.

Take pictures of myself drunk,
Keep them out of sight,
Learn to take flight from fight,
Start building barricades —

Between divided heart and softened brain,
Finally tell the different strains,

Keep them to their corners,
Keep them out of use,
No room for metaphor to unfurl or confuse.

Remember me, as you were, holding my hand,
Battling the guts of a snow storm in some foreign land.

SPACES

Spaces in between the door and floor,
Wooden slats slid over symbols etching,

Evenings stretching, please,

When I have loved you from my knees,
And when you're standing next to me.

NAVIGATING A TERRIFYING PARADISE

WORDS JUMPED OFF THE PAGE

Words jumped off the page,
Buttery veins running arterial roads to vulgar brains —
Cathedrals built from paragraphs,
Wrinkled paths began to intersect and stretch into the unknown,
Where I could unlearn what I'd been shown.

Stress lines in my heart,
Tiny earthquakes rattled and ripped apart —
How love can come by to collect our shards
And then leave us behind for a better path.

Scar tissue fabric, the cocoon shatters,
Perhaps I was not made for this, but made for something greater.

With pre-scripted noise
This timid temper quells and fades, and I exchange
The currency of youth for the certainty of age —

Spread new life on apartment walls,
Sit between supporting beams and watch as the world begins to fall.

POLLUTION

Manifested world, against my will and so it carries me, through landscapes built of bleary clouds and wheels propelled to an abyss of bright

White light, hands held out like sacrificial lambs to the sensation of your skin beneath them and between the walls of every room we fell into like

Night could not come soon enough.

Twists and coils of reality stretch out, forked roads to choose between, flipping coins on the edge of eternity — you keep your tail between your legs,

Death begs the end of us — though survivable, I place the frozen statue of our love on a shelf somewhere I cannot see or reach,

Teach me each lesson slowly, so I remember, so I move on through throngs of dreams — wiping distraction from my eyes, for the first time there's perception

Collecting direction to go on.

VANILLA

Vanilla orchid flower, blooming for a single day — so quick to embrace fate, to give itself away — and gentle against sunsets fade, closing up to die this way — bereft of any energy, or anything left to say —

Reflected in eyes cast too wide, brimming with high tide — let the rivers cry, let the sand and streets of your cheeks know the devastating flood of grief brought up from the well inside.

While petals pasted haphazardly back onto our rose, piece by piece, re-clothed — keep creating art to show, we're making pain seem beautiful —

Under a moon, cautiously half-full with patience, waiting. Should we ever bloom again.

SCAFFOLD

This morning, I flew home over roads, like arteries — uncomfortable magic, see, how the weight of my love for you sits inside of me.

Flying into sunset, settled soft on a city built from sand, under naive hands and how they shift the grains to form new land.

So, I looked out through egg shaped windows, scraped skies embrace the plane — the erections of buildings bondage wrapped in scaffolding and dozy cranes —

There's always something new to obscure the view, keep us distracted — crawl to a survivable distance and hope the bomb shelter protects us.

NAVIGATING A TERRIFYING PARADISE

EARTHQUAKES UNDERNEATH

Earthquakes underneath, most we don't feel — edifice rising out of the wilderness years; thirty blocks from here, where the forest becomes trees — the promise of adolescence crumbles into fear —

And what we're left with, this language of anguish — a search for a purpose both fruitless and desperate — I knew this, I know this — no wrong way to live this — plumb the depths of mediocrity as we try to outrun this.

Better to burn out, they say, as they watch me fade away — you hollow out somewhere safe, I'm cast out as a stray — your face does not look the same, while I feel no shame — you hang your disgrace like a shroud on your frame —

Where once you were a character, now you're just a name.

PART FOUR

ALONG DAINTY LINES WE WALTZ A WITTY REPARTEE,

MY SUMMER RACONTEUR BECOMES MY WINTER MEMORY

AUTUMN

Streets on fire with auburn decoration — shaken loose to fall to death — so, I collect them — safe in wicker basket townhouses, only meters from the gutter.

I rise with the moon and leave with the tide, pinning my past to the walls of a demolition site.

An absence of breath, all that I left with — a heartbeat laid like concrete across the breadth of my chest width.

SLEEP DEBT

A few years behind in repaying my sleep debt,
In the medium distance, planes escape to the sunset.

Intentions laid like train tracks,
In the space between our houses,
Overgrown by time
And its relentless context.

A few battles away from picking up your sword —
What would your bravery look like if you put action to thought?

Caught my finger in the doorway
When I left the room on Tuesday,
A few months passed quickly,
Yet the bruise chose to still stay.

A few times a day we connect at our soles
When the sun gets too high, we start to feel old.

Shadows I remember
From May to December,
We captured lightning
And burnt to death in the embers.

SKULL

Opened up my skull,
Took my brain out for a walk —
Seat of my soul.

And it's raining, and it's pouring,
And my skin is growing mould.

Thought about what quotes
I'd put on the graves of friends —

Could fill a week;
Inscribing Wingdings and then trying to sing them,

While I'm waiting to grow old
Getting ready for the end,
Waiting for the hourglass
Or the crush of the pendulum.

TANGO

Clouds make leopard print patterns on the ocean, claim the sky — blue and white, water and engine — they can have it, I don't mind — fingers twist thick paper into screwdrivers, nails tap oxygen mask warning signs.

I am fraught with frenetic energy, life's eternal, off-key symphony playing the beat of what you mean to me — how the key changes come so fast — so if I could get this message through — Well,

How lucky I have been, only now and then, to have my life interrupted by love.

Tango, and we two move through the pages of our story, hand in hand — stepping on each other's feet, again, in prior practiced turns that we still don't understand —

Around corners, we burn heels on dancefloors, if we could take no prisoners and leave this world behind, I wish we would.

FABRIC

From the fabric of your life,
I rip my stitching.
My wounds pine in gored defeat,
I collect them —
Scatter the leftovers to winter,
A skyline in silhouette, seen from the shore.

A rib cage rising from the sand dunes,
I seek shelter in the bone structure of friends,
The weather is inside me now,
Whether the storm will ever end.

GARDEN #2

I may sit forever
Among my Gladioli and my Aster
My Roses and my candles.

Sigh in the strains of music
That you could not quite compose for me.

Though I took you in, all the same.

NAVIGATING A TERRIFYING PARADISE

BLEACHERS

Man-made concrete bleachers claimed and sculpted by the waves — those fishbones spat up by the ocean, (though it claims it does not know quite what to do with them) — laying traps for innocent toes.

Murky water riptides, photographed through hollow driftwood — soldier crabs that move in sheets and retreat at the slightest sound — if I could follow them forever down the horseshoe bay to home,

Where I cannot come to any harm not self-inflicted — or measured carefully on scales of those carcasses of fish —

But, some squall brews on the horizon
And the boys are being boys again —

The thunder cannot be avoided, can only be endured.

WAKING UP

Waking up slowly —
A morning so delicious my eyes can taste the sweetener.

Colours blend richly—
Through the honeycomb lens of a security window.

Drops of sweat freeze dried—
Squeezed through clenched and clammy pores all night.

Blanket brushes skin—
Twisted among pale limbs exposed to unobserved shadows.

Whatever comes now—
Head spinning with the nausea of memory, waking up slowly.

IN CONVERSATION

In conversation with the leaves,
Ivy script in tendrils over cold stone —
Rips in my fingertips from opening old wounds,
Redesigning tissue to make new maps on my heart —
That's a start, reply the leaves,
In quiet condolence.

Under the conventional wisdom of owls,
Who swear
The moon will give her guiding beams —
It only tires me, these days.

What perfume could return memories
I lock in cabinets,
And throw away the keys.

HEIGHT OF SUMMER

Mountains pasted like wallpaper on the skyline, still, and coloured hues of purple — blues, and the burble of the lake with its medium-fast paced rush.

Disrupting flecks of sunshine dropped, haphazard, from above.

What the height of summer gave me, freckled shoulders — a little older, new perspective growing like the ducklings Spring has left the ducks with —

Sheltered under lace willow tree curtains, reaching to ripple water's surface.

I walk on steps of musical tones, fed through my ears to sink into my bones — found home in the distance between us, on the periphery of the seasons —

Blue sky and the patter of the sun — life to be lived, not fought or won. But an honour to be nominated —

For what the height of summer gave us.

MORNING OF JUST ME

In the morning solitude,
Spider webs creep toward eaves,
Sounds depart the breeze
To rest in nooks of waking ears.
As sunbeams template light on leaves,
Eyes turn inward to bygone years,
To wander roads that could have been,
On this morning of just me.

PART FIVE

A WINCE EVOLVED INTO AN EARTHQUAKE,
WAIF OF A WOMAN, REBUILT IN STONE.

HAIR

The strangest before and after I have ever been a part of.
I used to be pretty.
Did you know and never tell me?
Did you forget? If so, forgive me.

I got so skinny when I stopped eating,
Spent all my time at your feet and bleating,
Where did you always go?
Where were you, ever, though?

So,

I cut my hair after you,
Felt the rage like a reason to wake up.
Like the veins in my eyelids before makeup.

I cut my hair after you.

Pushed myself back to the righteous left,
After the flaccid centre you dragged me to.

ACKNOWLEDGEMENTS

Thank you to Vanessa Dreme for your fantastic editing job and feedback and Shoaib for the beautiful cover design and assistance with formatting.

www.ingramcontent.com/pod-product-compliance
Lightning Source LLC
Chambersburg PA
CBHW060621080526
44585CB00013B/937